Poet and novelist Lars Amund Vaage was born in 1952, grew up on a farm in western Norway and trained as a classical pianist. His fiction includes the award-winning novel *Syngja* (Sing, 2012) about a writer father and his autistic speechless daughter, the short-story collection *Den vesle pianisten* (The Little Pianist, 2017), and *Det uferdige huset* (The Unfinished House, 2020). Among other awards he has won the Gyldendal Prize, the Nynorsk Literature Prize and the Dobloug Prize for his life's work. *The Red Place* is Vaage's third poetry collection from Shearsman.

Lars Amund Vaage

THE RED PLACE

a poem

translated by
Anna Reckin with *Hanne Bramness*

Shearsman Books

First published in the United Kingdom in 2020 by
Shearsman Books Ltd
PO Box 4239
Swindon
SN3 9FN

Shearsman Books Ltd Registered Office
30–31 St. James Place, Mangotsfield, Bristol BS16 9JB
(this address not for correspondence)

www.shearsman.com

ISBN 978-1-84861-711-7

ACKNOWLEDGEMENTS
The publisher thanks Forlaget Oktober for permission
to publish this English translation of *Den raude staden*.

Some of these translations first appeared in translation in *Osiris* 87 (2018), and
NOON: journal of the short poem 16 (2019); our thanks to the editors: Andrea
Moorhead and Philip Rowland.

Anna Reckin would like to acknowledge the substantial contribution made to
this work by Hanne Bramness for the Norwegian; especially in its final stages,
this work has been the result of a close and fruitful collaboration.

This translation has been published with the financial support of
NORLA (Norwegian Literature Abroad).

The Red Place

THERE IS A YOUNG MAN inside me
I see him standing
by a dark wall
somewhere in the forest
Light from the fjord
is trickling through
Who has chased this youth
out into the open?
He says not a word
has nothing to tell
He is standing on the far side
of a trail
by a wall made of wattle
or rotten timber
He is standing there, lean
and strong
His hands open
His bike thrown aside
nearby
He might have brought gifts with him
or messages about where we come from
but things and time
are not his concern

WHEN JUST NOW I said
there is a young man inside me
I would also say:
I do not envy him
I am not happy to see him
nor do I mourn him
I do not approach him
and will not greet him
This is not the time for words
He can stay behind
He is only some youth
I met today in the forest
The forest that grows
inside me
I caught a glimpse of him
Then I let my gaze wander
over the ridges
and gaily
walked on

BUT IN THAT instant
I saw the young man move
he stirred into life
in the moment before
he disappeared
Maybe it was I
who left him first
but then
he too was keen to get away
from me
or maybe he just
dissolved
into life after death
or time
gone by
I saw
that he ran
or fled, at least
he moved on
flapping his way
out of my life
I did not stop him
not wanting to think
about him any more
but I could not
deny
he had left
a stain
on the wall behind where
he stood
invisible black, invisible

white, a
watermark
a sting
on the
inner eye

I CAN STILL see the young man
as he leaves me. What he disappeared into
– a forest, a world – is also gone
It closed itself off, was emptied
of memory while I
sat there still living
I do not know
how great my loss
He jumped on his bike
was soon through the forest
and somewhere in town, an area with houses
and people I have never
met. But there is
a darkness which is white
It shines empty
of objects, where I still see
that young man, little
glimmers of him. A hand
or foot
rising out of
moss

SOMETIMES I SEE real
young people. They come dancing
out of the edges of the forests or from
bedrooms or bathtubs or
school buses where they
are packed together the way words
lie waiting under
the larynx or gather
themselves up into penholders
or behind the soft
computer screens
The young people come
they are jumping around
showing off
all their limbs
and muscles which simply
want to stretch and lift
They have not lost
childhood in their
movements, but have kept
the free pull of
the skin and the dimples
at their hips. They
are not yet
grown-up
autists like me
who only have movements
resembling something
else

I HAVE ANOTHER young man
on the outside
I pulled him along
throwing him on like a jacket
as I ran out
Now he is stuck to my skin
I pass through the dark area
behind the ramshackle outhouse
What before was a small field
has become a dumping ground for garden plants
I pass over the wire fence
cross the narrow tarmac road
and go out into what will be the pasture
for spring has found a place in me
I take a deep breath
all the way down to my roots
My jacket is grey
The edge of the woods is drawing near
comes to meet me
Birdsong can be heard from the trees
My skin is smooth
my eyes keen
my step easier
each day

THERE IS A YOUNG MAN here with me tonight
He is sitting over by the stove
Why have I not noticed him before
He is plant-like, tree-like, bows down
hides what is innermost in him among the leaves
He counts how old he is
with his fingers and toes
and sings without words of a time that did not come
things that will never come to pass
He has not come to keep me company
A boundary crosses the room
a line, a grave
He doesn't look at me
doesn't know I exist

THE YOUNG PEOPLE hang in the air
floating in the clear blue
youngsters, cherubs, weightless
invisible. The young people are ready to burst
brittle as ripe fruit
bulging with invisible juice
The young people are not dreaming, not
descending, they will not be landing
for a long time yet
The sun shines on the young
some will say
It will take them away
out of the firmament

MOTHER WENT to the red place
with grand gestures
as if she had made up her mind
but it was not so
Mother went to the red place
and passed through it
She did not notice she had been there
When she had come out on the other side
she immediately went to another red place
She went from one red place to another
passing through them all
The red places formed a ribbon
round her life
Mother held this ribbon together
with grand gestures
and a will to live
The red places were a burning necklace
around mother's life
Mother fell from her childhood
through the red places
which hung from the sky
Mother fell through the red places
while she went from one to another
Mother fell in toward her own hot, red centre
while she carried out
the grand gestures
Mother fell and moved around in a circle
which was impossible
Finally she found herself in a red place
She found a haven in a red rest-home
There she sat
inside the red place
Her feet would go no further

IT IS NOT the dead I see come to the wood's edge
I stand where I often stand, behind me the steep cliff
rises, and before me the green plain, grey
with dew. To the other side is a stone wall
built by the old ones and the woods stretching
toward the distant sea. Did not the dead say
that they would come like this someday, did they not promise
me this in a dream, a vision, a feeling
that nothing will pass? Life does not die
but changes shape, they said, this sleepless night
I stand motionless, see them coming through an opening
in the wall where it fell down in times no one remembers
see them coming out of the woods, also steadily
drawing nearer, wanting to reclaim the plains
They are the dead. They must have gathered
somewhere, not in the woods, not on the pink forest floor
but further in. First they sank into the ground
and woke lonely in the kingdom of the dead
they have never been so lonely, all they had loved
they had left behind, involuntary. Thus many years passed
but they must have found each other, they must
have recognized each other, and got together
in new ways, with other loves than are
revealed to the living. They must have rubbed off against each other,
melted into one another. For they share the same hair, same skin
and bodies, facial expressions, the same age
I can see that. They have cancelled out the distinctions
between themselves and the other dead, here they come
like wild animals who no longer want to linger
in the forest, but are teeming forward, into the green, the open
that is colourless, morninglike, now
almost out on the plain, they are one
creature, one body, one circle, hear

them humming, singing, they dance, do not turn
toward me, but are gazing and gazing at each other
How could I think
they would come to me

I WAS HERE before the land
I come with the boat
and think this
Islands, holms, flies
shivering in the windowpanes, quivering
in the noise from the engine
I was here first
it occurs to me
before the rocks, the water
and the salt
of the oceans. I
was here, a silent
seed, a poor codlin
among the planets
in the magnetic fields
this stagnation

THE LAND DREW itself over me
the sea-scoured rocks pressed themselves
under me
The high-speed ferry shot straight
into me. The ocean
lay on top of me
A small thought
an insignificant phenomenon
I was here first
and will also be
the last to leave

I AM in the land
Not in the steep crags
Not in the high-rise houses
disgorging themselves onto the hillsides
Not in the hot-air balloons
loudly announcing the price of meat
over the cities
I am in the pieces of paper
which shift
when a small animal passes
I am in the tree
which stands shivering
beyond the bend
off the footpath
I am in the stone edging
in the raspberry roots
even further in
in what nobody sees
and where no one treads
in the moss, in the soil
in the dust, in nothing
I am in the land
The land is in me

A YOUNG MAN MAKES music inside me
with his slender limbs
and his wild heart

At night I can hear him sing
locked up in himself

He wants to play what he does not know
He wants to play that which makes it
impossible for him to play

He will pave a way
in the forest of hope and memory
and spring out naked
between the song and the instrument
And the instrument will be the song

He wants everything to be easy
All he has to do is to lift his hand
and the instrument will sound
He knows this is impossible
But he still wants it

He wants to join the other young people
through the instrument
The instrument must be him
his being
nothing should
stand in the way

A CHILD I have lost laughs
inside me
I heard it just now, today
when I was reminded
of my blindness
yet again

A child I have lost
called out from long ago
Perhaps the child will approach me
if I sit long enough
on this hidden stool

Is this the child I shall write about
This dead child that is me

Are there no children
who need it more

I CAN IMAGINE many places
mother might have gone
I see her performing
new gestures
in a strange land
which is also the old one

She might have walked slowly
away from the forgotten house
with the blue door
and the yellow wall
the newly seeded flower beds
all around

She might have laid aside
all those practical tasks
I do not see
Now all I can see is this
putting something aside
The most beautiful thing I know

I could have seen
an impulse come to mother
for freedom, laughter
a hidden pattern
could have emerged
Something of no importance

She might have turned
to what never existed
such as what I see now
Wet grass, a small
ditch, rotten sticks
green, yellow, shadow

I see mother leave
so slowly that
she is almost standing still
Then she speeds up again

WHEN AT LAST I will say
what I could not before
those foul words
I could not wring out of me
words forbidden
or unborn
in the throat's nursery

When I see a new word
coming across the fields
through parks, restaurants, bars
with long strides
and what I did not know
that I could drink
quenches my thirst
so bitterly, so hot

Then I think fear
has left me
for I open a dictionary
I never stumbled on before
But it is too late
for my mouth to cut out
songs and curses
it had always lived without

Time and wind
cross my lips
rampage at the back of my throat
until the spit dries
and sticks my tongue to my teeth
where words die

Nobody has told
me that time
kills. Afterwards
I was told
I should have
seen this for myself

The word that has been lying waiting
fades away
and what remains
is what I left unsaid

IS IT NOT father who comes walking there?
I hear the song he always whistled
The song and father are one
Father comes and goes in the same movement
He does not look at me
He does not come to me
It is I who can either follow him
or let it be
He can pull me with him
or pass me by
Father is not coming
he is not going
He comes from a place
and will return to that same place
Father is not going to a place
he is going to work
He is walking along the edge of a bog
It was his father before him who worked the bog
Father walks doubled over, looks down
He is not studying the tussocks, the hollows
or the worms in the bog
He walks to what he has let go
He goes to what he is not
He bends over the work
his muscles stretch
and he whistles inside me

FATHER STANDS in the muck cellar. He stands in shit
He stands in what he does not love
He does the work he cannot manage
He lets go of work into work
He drops work into a grey hole
He empties work of work
He stands bent over in the muck barn
Inside him is a young man
who never changed

ANOTHER MAN comes walking
from the other side
of a mountain, a land
we do not know
He is not inclined to
provide descriptions
of what we do not understand
and is in no hurry
to sing
In the beginning
there were no words
simply nothing
and he has picked this up,
this man
He comes along
the old road
creating many small things
with his eyes

WHERE DID the other man get the clothes
underneath which he was naked
The little hat, the green jacket
the embroidered ribbon he left behind
so that he could find
his way home again
He brought sunshine
into the kitchen and said that
the grass was green
and birds sang for reasons
he wanted to explain
We gathered round him
pulled up frail chairs
He loosened tied tongues
so new sentences could come forth
from the women, and the old people
who could not laugh
scraped their long-forgotten cheeks
till they bled
Was it me accompanying my father
between the houses
when the man had waved goodbye
Was I the one who carried my father in my mind
into the dark cowshed
I who lime-washed the old wall
so that it would be bright
for us and the animals

TODAY I SEE the inner eye hang like a burnt-out lamp
over this landscape I do not recognize
What dark hills, gorges, stony fields are these
What transitions between sea and endlessness
The inner eye, grey from uncertainty, from doubt
hovers between buildings where nobody lives
work buildings, deserted schools, purged
of wall charts of foreign countries
the human nervous system, the skeleton
It seems as if the history of human development
is completed. The inner eye
goes from door to door it does not need to open
It dozes, it is shut, does not exist, does
not see, it sees the only thing
which has not got stuck inside
beneath the abdominal wall
nor set down
on paper or in mental constructs
Unquiet, the inner eye searches for rest
It will never open
For it is the closed which opens
in this grey world, it is blindness that sees
what is newly painted
with no colour, only a little darker
than white. Now the inner eye approaches
the soul. It lies by that wall
also grey
It is arches, bulges and tubes
It lives, breathes, maybe it will burst
It resembles intestines
or a plucked goose

A CHILD PLAYS inside me
The child has found its way
to the cold hard piano
Now the child is playing
soundlessly

THE CHILD COMES to the piano
from a forgotten place
The piano was lifted in
but not the child
The reason for this is lost

CAN A CHILD be born
in the gleam of a shining tree
or come running
to the sound
that dissolves the moment

CAN THE CHILD see itself, the child
inside the child, in the sound
the small fingers make
as they click out of the moment?

CAN I WRITE of what is not
that which dropped away
leapt out of sight
flew off before morning
or never came and settled
Something not given to me
not made by the soil
not reaped from plenty
or sewn fast in the memory
of those standing around me
There is an empty space
a dark area
Is that why I turn
away from you
while our ties become weaker
and the children grow
I look far away
for a dead landscape
a reversed longing
a parting not kept to
clothes that were not laid out
the journey which did not start
the train which did not run
the moment I should have seen you

I WAS to blame
for when they came and asked me to come along
I said no and ran off
through gaps in light and shade
beyond the yellow summer's day
into an empty outhouse
dusk damp in the corners
There I sat for a long time
by the wall which let the daylight in
waiting for them to come back
and ask me again
If they had
and I don't believe they would have done
my answer would have been the same

I HAD TO GET UP in the end
and go. Outside I could see
that the summer evening had opened up
hardened
Quietly I passed into that area of darkness
which does not exist

STRAIGHT AWAY I was surrounded by animals
sheep and cows so startled
they had forgotten all they knew
They had lost all they had been taught, no
longer cared about what they liked so much
the green pastures, the quiet groves
of alder and hazel. They were running
back and forth, kicking with hind feet, bellowing
they turned and ran again, and I
ran with them

I WAS TOLD there was a law
against running after animals
Harsh words about duty and good sense
Had I not learnt this at home
they asked
I could not remember
even if I opened my memory
all the way down to my heart's floor
what was missing in me
was not there

I PLAY BACH at the funeral of a good friend
I go to the piano and see time dissolve
It trickles through the mesh of days
so that the mourners tremble with unfamiliar hope
I sit and wait, feel that I am a child again
The signs on the score mercilessly hide
the sounds to come
As I am about to play I hear Bach
in a flash. He comes with the songs
of the cathedrals where I have been
The songs chase each other like animals in the forest
they leap and jump, the movements change
but the animals stay the same, mysterious, their animal hearts
burst when the flight ends
and the great musician receives the applause
Now I am the one playing
I have struck the first chord
Not to think is good advice, rather forget
the wise man in the coffin
Not to be in mourning. But still to be present
The body will remember the notes. That
is a wild hope. But today
neither up nor down
good nor bad
beautiful nor helpless
has any meaning
they never did
I watch the coffin being lifted, floating out
and hear how frail music is
I too am lifted, sway likewise
My hands scramble over the keys
creeping blindly from bar to bar
There is a bridge of sound

and something to hold on to if we feel dizzy
It is necessary to build invisible towers
we can climb
so we can look ahead
to the old meeting-place of life and air
Then the music is over

THERE ARE FRIENDS we have never met, and will never talk to
other than in single words: thanks, for example, to the one who
steps aside by an entrance and holds the door open
Unknown friends meet here, in this hall before me, with its honey-
        coloured light
Why have we come and gathered here, pressed so close together?
We do not know
It is only this moment that counts
and this room with its high ceilings
The light fades lowest down on the walls
under the rows of chairs, behind the curtains, by the doors
which have now been closed
We talk to one another. Some are alone, keep quiet
The sound of voices rising, amplified by the walls and ceiling
becomes a choir, not intentionally, but by chance
Quiet words are exchanged. Perhaps something important is mentioned
We do not listen to the choir. We are the choir. It envelops us
setting at a distance all that is not this one thing, here and now
At one point the lights are dimmed, the chorus of voices is hushed
until a new, deep quiet prevails
Silence binds us together. It is afternoon
A man has come in at the front
A small man in a grey suit
He is looking down
No one saw him enter. No one saw the door open
He has moved away from the wall, taken a few steps out
Where did he come from? What does he want here
All eyes are on him. Everyone is waiting for him
He is unaware of this
He is alone. He has come here alone. He has been alone
in a room behind the stage, or further away, out
by a border, in a different country, among the poor
He has been to war zones, among refugee camps

He has seen suffering there. He has tried to help
but it had little effect.
An abyss of distress
He walks by the wall
Lifts his hand, strokes the panelling
Now he stops, picks at something, a broken piece
The piece is something inside him.
Something he picks at in order to forget or endure
It costs him a good deal to walk
With each step comes a new thought
Still he walks on
The walls keep silent. The floor keeps silent
The man does not look at us. He has not come to us
He does not care about us. He has other duties
Is there anyone else he is looking for, or is there nobody? Does
            no one wait for him
He is unknown, one in a crowd, on an open street
He has run errands, bought cabbage, potatoes
most importantly wine
He comes on foot, burdened, empty-handed
in transit, he gazes on us
without purpose, without history
And then he sits down and plays

IN ANOTHER CONCERT HALL, another man comes running onto
     the stage
He throws himself at the instrument, half-seated
stretches out his hands
in among the keys, the strings, the hammers
plugs himself into the great, black body
tears the notes out in clumps of sound, the rattle
of footsteps on stairways, making turns, small pauses, a shower
of thoughts left over, something resembling grief, anger, more scales
He flings himself in even further, as far as the tuning-pins
he glides across the floor of the case, races
all the way down to the feet, the pedals
far into the wood, wanting to fill each timber with life
He is running into himself, through the small holes
he once drilled, the roads he blasted through mountains
back then, when he was a child
He is rushing downwards, into the time
when he lived like this, inside tones, nothing else
could make up for what he lacked, no happiness
could carry him to the soundscape, that familiar place
where he could float, suspended
A promised land he could see
He had seen it many times before
But now this land is closed to him
He has finished the first piece, runs from the stage
waits in a white room, as in a hospital, after an operation
on a lover or a friend. But he cannot wait
swallowing the gap between him and the instrument, he flies across
the landscape of the concert hall
gazing about him wildly, he is a crow, he comes flapping
and settles on the stool. He walks from bar to bar on weary feet
tired, grey from all the hours of practice
and all the joy he once found in playing

He has chased us under the seats, down onto the floor
we are pulled back toward the stage, out again
on to the assembly-line of the great music machine
Our thoughts rise, are dust and steam
forming columns of daylight within crumbling walls
We are outside or in, another place
for we too yearned for notes that did not come
today, other than as a slide and swarm
a near-void
Now it is over
the applause resembles pool sounds
children throwing a ball far off
In the hall a white rain falls
We get up, have started to leave
Then the man comes in again, wants to play more
No one has asked him
He plays slowly, without obligation
He plays what he had planned to give
We are pulled toward this dark gentleness
The hall disperses into human rivers
The rows of chairs scattered, a rich yield of ashes
and the railing by the stage melts away
We stand close by the instrument's wall
while the old man plays on

NOW THE CHILD may come
you say
But I will not let the child through
I am the keeper of the child
I let it stay
in obscurity

I RUN FAST through the forest
I have been told
that somewhere far ahead
God is waiting
The child
is at my heels

WHERE IS THE CHILD, I ask myself
as I stand on the farthest headland
I have a view
straight out into the ocean
I have outrun the child
who did not exist

IT WAS I who told you about the child
At my signal you now call
for the child
A way opens between you and the child
But the child is hiding
in me

THE STORY I TOLD was not new
You knew it all from before
Even so you forgot the child
Therefore I must defend the child
against your love

ONE DAY THE CHILD will come to you
Then my story will have
lain down on the grass
while what I did not say
rages across the landscape
far away

YOU, child
What song will you hear
so the road ahead
does not fall apart
on your tongue

ONE DAY I shall fetch the child
out of the empty house
See, we are going
a long way far out into the marshes
The law changes
with each step

MY STORY
tore you apart
so the child
awoke in you
Where was your story?

WHERE IS YOUR child now
untold as it is
Perhaps it is running free
Why did your story not come
before mine

MY CHILD lost me
among the brown shadows
that forgotten day
Now I ask just as much for myself
as for the child
Let my words
live in you

MANY YEARS LATER I went to the house where mother lived
I came down the road, opened the door
Mother was not there. I ask
Can a house become invisible
torn down so not even the site
shows up in the grey heather

Can a house slide off a steep hill
be swallowed by the sands, be one
with the sea, or is it light
that wipes the house out

I entered the living room
Although she was gone, mother was there
Her things were clean
orderly, laid out
Everything planned by the forces of life
birth, still lingering

I knew at once where she had gone
Sometimes she took herself off
somewhere quieter
wordless neighbourhoods
that opened up to her

Then she walked by the roadside
in the grass and scrub
which grew invisible

or no longer existed
just as the house too was floating
on the edge of the real

Mother went to her other house
a higher place
a bare building
a silent structure
from where she could see the main road
Who would come
who would leave
and those who never appeared

I followed her in
through the doors she had opened
and saw that she was standing or sitting
on the floor, far off
by a non-existent wall

I met her gaze
filled with light and water
a coastline, cracked rock, a scrap of wood
and the stormy sky

MOTHER IS dead
and a new freedom has sprung up
I who do not even believe
that the soul flies out of the body
when the worms come
wonder
Is this the same freedom
that coursed through me
once upon a time when I ran
with small clenched fists
in the warm, dark wind?
Words, words, words – I should have collected them up
from my body, my life
and put them together freely
in a pattern no one had seen
but recognized at once
Blinded I walk
along the ditch with yellow flowers
cannot lift my eyes
above the great forest which hides
what I have lost

MOTHER DID NOT WALK towards the green, but went through it
She dashed along roads
still unmapped
with animals leaping up
branches swinging aside
She went up to bland, gaudy
glitzy wallpaper and the shelves in food shops
and crashed her way through
It was impossible to know if she was coming or going
had left us or was returning
or if it was the pace she loved
and how she moved her arms as she swam in the air
I followed her, felt the sting in my lungs
as we ran aimlessly
not from house to house
but out on the slopes and gashes
where animals had not trodden for years
but the sun shone and warmed the mountains
She walked through a hole in time
A distance came between us
I remember mother, far up the hill
she was headed towards ridges of rusted lumber
and yesterday's bread, so far off
that trees and bushes were like brush strokes against the sky
Cuckoo clocks, inherited pictures, crystal bowls
did not matter high up there. Mother's feet
clipped the brambles and flew
over the hidden rocks
I was there and not there, as was usual
A son must always come or go
with the same feeling of being tied down
or forgotten
I lost speed, my steps would not follow

in mother's footprints. My thoughts would not settle
on her. I no longer detected the scent
of bodies and lefse from the inmost courtyards
The tiny rooms could not contain
mother's family running back
through the generations
I did a backwards somersault
tumbled down the staircase, swerved round corners
could not keep track of time rushing
out into the small field
with turnips, swedes, these now checked in their growth, wilting
The autumn is too cold, the foliage is limp
eaten through by worms. Nothing came from the attempt
to grow something, create something of our own
pull together the barest livelihood
Eventually I met mother again
She had ended up in a village with blue light
She was finished with all the green
which had never really caught her attention
I cannot recall
who sent me a letter about mother
who was sitting on a ridge with a view of a wall
she thought I had built, and wanted to know
why the stones were laid out before her in such a way
that she could move neither foot nor finger
Quiet had come over her
Peace had eaten its way into her
an unwelcome feeling
I had the call-up letter in my hand
there should have been no need for such a letter
My skin was tanned from all the work
outdoors. I came
to the hospital with heavy shoes
and had to force my way through the doors
I was more grown up than mother, taller

than the hills where she had flown
Her tiny pupils chased
from one wall to another
Did she close up time inside me
or did she try to chase away death
I was back home again
Everything was as it was before
I did not manage
to comfort her

SOMEWHERE in father's body
past autumn-coloured alveoli
in among pink membranes
stretching down towards hollows
above pale organs
through the vascular paths
that branch amongst tight
quiet musculature
there is a small glen
where animals graze

YOU CAN GO back in time
turn and take the path you came by
Steer against the wind
don't give up if the elements refuse
Just chase the hours back into the clock
You can turn your body inside out
so that once again you become small and blunt
and meet your own weeping
and your gasping laughter
You can go down smaller
than your childish body
You can shrink
invade the warm darkness
where you press yourself
all the way into the black hole
You can crawl through the impossible
Inside the ganglions
you can burst into gametes
You can set yourself free, fly
into other parts of the body
or into the animal kingdom. Remember you are heading home
Now you can enter another body
You can split yourself
out into this one body
or several
leave their destinies
race down and away alongside time
or distances. Now to spread
into the world where ancestry fades
They leap into the bushes
and grow smaller, blink and die
into themselves
rolling further into gatherings of fathers, groups of mothers

that again go back to the beginning
This is how you arrive at the magnificently small
You can see the grandeur of grey
the beautiful, ugly buildings
the rich, poor rooms
There is a cradle in a corner
and underneath it you will find
a grief that has not been named

HOW WAS IT with father and the horse
Was it father who followed the horse
into the small hazel forest
where the horse completely vanished
Or did the horse go away from us of its own accord
and shrink away out of melancholy
until it was the size
of a rat
Was it perhaps the small grey tractor
father drove into the same thicket
where the horse disappeared
The tractor
became a rock or shadow
or an earth-coloured spot
next to a tree trunk
Or did father drive the tractor into the sea
where it stood spinning
with water above the lights
until the engine sounded like the scuffle of crabs' feet
And was it not really a red tractor
that tossed father up
into the air when he tried
to pull up the old root that neither
the horse nor the old grey tractor had managed to budge

FATHER is falling
he crashes, has thrown
himself out of the aeroplane
It is only a matter of
gravity and no
gravity, spirals
of thought race
into him
or out

The parachute opens
the jerk pulls him
up again
Father walks
the air, sees far
across the landscape
Does not feel
at home

ONE DAY mother and I
were as small as each other
or as large
This can often happen
in the room where death
comes visiting

VIOLET OR cardinal red
the colour of my heart
A flame burns there
I cannot quench
Now when I will soon forget words
I see myself
young and bent over
in a landscape I cannot recognize

I CAME TO the white or grey gates
which no one could be bothered to watch anymore
My face rigid from ashes and caresses
I descended into that part of eternity
where humans still swam
and waited to find a rock
they could hold on to
I sat down some distance from the bed
and read books which described a love
that grew inwards
with a festering wound
I tried to concentrate on
what I had understood
while what I could not explain
was there in the room
I recognized from long ago
I did not approach
until the breath took a pause
one which lasts till this day
Then I took some steps toward the grave
felt how relief
seared my lungs
I ran out to the others
shouting out about human dignity
and how I could change myself
be more fully attuned
They had come and gone
at a point in time
which broke up the mysteries into assertions
that did not exist
I placed my hand on your brow
and felt the warmth
turn to air

I LIKE THAT time of day when words quieten down
At last they find their place among the sounds
of things that crawl in ceilings and walls
and float far away
There is a dry haze between people
They close the doors that are kept open
against the yellow air
I don't ask where the cat is
and don't need a list to jog my memory
No one moves along shop shelves
or approaches the ovens with melted flesh
Maybe there is a tingle in the groin
shutting down the need to explain
Kitchen stools scrape back
Cars wait at gates
The houses have stopped growing, breathe out
There is a world far down, under the furniture
which the bugs do not notice
Nooks and crannies beg for help
to be filled with hope
No one needs to work
only fingertips will move
the last things
Do humans still form words?
Sharpen your ears for all the tiny things that fly
in the light
Words go around quietly among humans
who sit unmoving
Words move around as humans did once
they take on their gestures
Shyness makes humans lower their eyes
when mouths kiss
vowels

NOW WHEN I can see
the lane down to the copse
and the bend that I know hides
a white light
I want to play out
my youthful dream
Not to make it come true
Piano teachers left me
without discovering my quiet voice
or the fingers I stretched out
towards those other, happy children
Other musicians grew into freedom
Toppled the heavy instrument
which is like the muscle of the heart
over into people's open mouths
I play alone
Not to stay silent
has become my dream
Every day I enter among notes
which no one counts, no one
hears their trembling beats
against the axis of time

SEPTEMBER, sun
and I want to play more
although greater pianists than I
stand in the woods waiting
Even now I hear the incredible notes
they played yesterday
Still I put my hands forward
for inspection
It is important to turn away the debt collectors
who send out prizes
to reward those who stay small
And an old man is allowed to apply for
a place in a music kindergarten
After the meal he can run outside
as the starlings gather
It is September, and I will play
as I did the first few years
and the last days
I prefer to forget the time in between
with its rich, full chords
I did not reach
Who can put a price
on what the heart wants to sing
Don´t listen to the maestros
who place scarecrows
by the orchestra pits
I shall come onto the podium
find the only note
and lose it again

I CANNOT work out if I let the piano down
I often think about it
I was never pushed to play the piano
No one told me to practice
Still I was pushed
I pushed myself
or something pushed me
Something in myself pushed me
Did I push myself away from me?
I came across the bright plains
to the piano, which shone with another light
Inside the bright piano I pushed myself round and round in a circle
I pushed me away from the piano and into myself
I should have pushed me away from myself
I should have forgotten myself
Did I let the piano down or myself?

I CAME ACROSS the bright plains
The plains burned behind me
I consumed the plains with my hunger
The piano waited for me always
But I could not come to the piano
The piano waited, without a sound
for all who would come
Each and every one must create their own sound
The piano opened the door, but without a word
Where should one hang one's coat
Was there a place
for warming one's hands
The piano was dead

THE PIANO did not come to me
It had no wish to welcome me
because it did not know how
I came to the piano
and threw myself against it
whereupon it opened up all the way in
to its silent mechanisms
We emptied into each other
But emptiness
is a poor gift between lovers

THE PIANO ONLY LOVES the one who comes across the plains
The one who comes across the plains may love the piano
But the piano demands lifelong loyalty
and calm
Never again wander far from the keys
Speak with the piano every day
Build a nest under the lid
Let your unhappiness dwell
among the strings

FATHER HAS BEEN HANGING by a thread frayed thin from work
from the olden days until now
So many years have passed
Has father noticed?
He has become as small as an insect
in amongst hoes, spades and shovels
Father maybe does not remember everything about work
I think he has forgotten
why he was born on a farm
like this one
in an old house which sleeps
among rocks and spider webs
Oh father, father
Have you also forgotten
the youthfulness you thought
would never die

A THOUGHT HAS struck me
How the piano
with its fusion of metal
and wood and its kisses
inside the canals of the ear
can fill moments with light
Time can disappear
while I sit here
Another man can walk by
outside my small cabin
listening to this

SOMETIMES WE visit a big city
We walk along the streets
with naked shins
and bare heads
We are thinking in a language
no one understands
We have sudden spells of confusion
and ask each other things
everyone knows about
We feel free
for we don't have to carry our suitcases
we left them in our room at the hotel
We take in the memorials
and let them sink
into our unconscious
so we may change
Now we can walk on
to a quieter street
or stay in a park
for a while
Give us a quick glance
we are marked
by work that has been erased

NEXT MORNING I RUSH out into the city
not knowing
if I'll be free
or if I'll just buy breakfast
for my travel companions
I think I can make out the smell
of bakers' ovens
even though they cooled
several hours ago
I hurry on
along the housefronts, turning
where they turn
Now I am rising up
as if on a heavenly stairway
of everything I don't know
thinking I can translate this
into words of wisdom
later on that day

IN THE AFTERNOON I SIT in the back yard
on a chair I have taken out with me
I don't know if this is allowed
I can see rows of windows, great trees
within the city
Clothes-lines and flower-boxes
press gently around my frontal lobes
Nagging children
people quarrelling, laughing
kitchen appliances, spin-dryers, shrieks
from TV shows, faraway
cars, a train
make my vocal cords vibrate

FREEDOM, TAKE AWAY my history
no, freedom, take instead
all that is
around me, freedom, that
which closes in, that which is
homeland, freedom
throw it off, like clothes
or a pincer-grip on thinking
Freedom, to be alone
but not so much so
that no one comes to the pen
touching paper, freedom
let them come to me
those who do good
or harm, no
those who merely exist
Mark them
freedom
inside me

THERE IS a place
where strawberry plants gleam in the grass
and sugar peas wind around strings
saying that
times are more peaceful now
Consider the deep
blindness that shaped
the plants, and those
who dig the earth

THERE ARE valleys, with gently sloping
heights, built of something
unknown to you
And you can walk
the way the landscape sends you
There is gravel that lifts
the foot through the garden gate
and grass which grows beyond
the verges, making
a way in

AND THERE ARE houses where you find room
upon room and doors
you can choose freely
You enter
and think
as a dog might
by your foot
This is where I was headed

OTHER DAYS you count cobble stones
let out small words
which are alive. They have been clinging
to the one with whom you
hold hands

YET other
days you walk
alone
But you know
she exists, the one
who wants you to exist

BODY AND THOUGHT can be one
when you know
you are welcome

FATHER IS in another room
in the room
It is not walls, glass
or any air
that separates him from us
but distance
skin

CAN ONE COME further away from father
than father was
from his father?
He approached the mark he made
on the crust of the earth
asked him about the cultivation of stars

UNDER HIS CLOTHES father has
other clothes
under those clothes he has
metal ribs
wrapped in cotton
leather and plastic
Under all of this
heat builds up
Blood pumps
blood. I stand
behind on the tractor
see the grey clothes
The tractor too is grey
The smoke from father´s pipe
and the exhaust pipe
mingle
The dirt shovel
sways from
side
to side
The tractor holds
a steady course, the heavy
wheels do not seem
quite round, but
so slow
We shall never
see each other again

SHALL I ENTER the
empty rooms
after father has gone
They have long been
unused
Once they were moved
to a quieter place
in the village
I come to it
by accident
The door is glass
it flies open
by itself
My foot lifts by itself
and I go in
A young man
is sitting by the table
says he was ordered
to keep watch

WHEN I SIT and play
I think of father
Not because he listened to me
very often, or
encouraged me
but

Music, he said

Music
said father
nothing more
than that
and also
nothing less

Music is
far away from here
perhaps that is what he meant

FATHER SITS ON the tractor, bent over the steering wheel
facing forward
On the shield sits a neighbour, brother, maybe
a friend
Father accelerates
pushing and pushing
at the clutch
so the wheels spin
and mud and roots splash
behind him
The tractor bumps along, eating
its way into the evening
They are headed for music

TODAY FATHER IS dressed up
has put on a suit and tie
He stands alongside his father, his mother
and other relatives both big and small
He has his hands in his pockets
looks down and smiles
I hide
my serious child's face
against him

FATHER CREATED the landscape
at least he rolled out rocks
and pulled up roots
But the roots also pulled
him down toward them

I walk in the landscape
father shaped. Afterwards
he let it all grow over
and become as it was before

Where is father?
He is standing by the edge
of a bog. He has
blue clothes
and grey skin

I stand close by
him, as close
as I can come
without becoming him

He stands by me
outside of me
whistling notes
that don't exist

He lifts his head
toward the fells
they too
must fall

My poor, poor father

I WANT TO SEE father again
I want to reach him
and I follow him
out of the house
up the road
through time and space
to where the tools are, from
which he must choose

He is standing still
on his own ground
I walk up to him
It is raining ashes
and no wind comes

I should have said
poor father
but I have no words
no face

NOW THE LANDSCAPE rings
with metal and sun
The landscape so much wants
a voice

Who jumps so quietly
from peak to peak?
Who gnaws on roots
for breakfast?

What forest is this
which keeps quiet
about who you are

What sort of paper
lies there waiting
at our doors

TAKE A TRIP out
into the landscape. For this you must
understand

You don´t have
anything else

Father inherited it
and now
father is dead

Go out and see
father standing
in the gully
he made

Go down to father
along the path
men even older
hacked out of the stone

It is necessary to believe
that you can get
to father

Because the words were not there
that time when
you needed them

THERE WERE no words
Only that closed
mouth of yours

and that burning
empty
step, which
you could not take

There was nothing
behind the word
either
but deeper within
you sang

MEMORY IS a creature
living in the forest
One day it rolls over on its side
and dies

A quiet wind comes
and a wordless draught
which rips everything up
and lets the pieces float about
in air that is like water

Buildings are pulled apart
and the walls between days crumble
backwards in time
trickling down
over mountains

Your inner eye wanders
or hangs onto threads
of which you had no idea
and lights up a landscape
you ought to know

What you see is nothing
But the ones you loved
are standing by the edges
of what look like
houses and villages

You see a new connection
opening up between you
and those who have started walking away
from the homes they yearn for
to a new forest

You can see trees
no bigger than a toad
bid mother and father
goodbye

Your old face
which is young
wipes itself out
beyond the cheekbones
to a gentle beginning

Tear open the thought-bubble
pull apart the meeting-places
you saw
with eyes that were turned
away from humankind

Now you can stand
on the hill for a while
before you go
Leave your song out there
among the stones

Turn around, see
another song
a small child
curls up against you

And new waters come so quietly
to the gorges
where once you wandered

www.ingramcontent.com/pod-product-compliance
Lightning Source LLC
Chambersburg PA
CBHW022158080426
42734CB00006B/487